YOUNG DOC JAX
I WANT TO BE LIKE DOC JAMES!

BY KAI JACKSON
ILLUSTRATED BY CAMERON WILSON

Young Doc Jax
I Want To Be Like Doc James!

Fifth Ribb Publishing
6951 Olive Blvd
St. Louis, Missouri, 63130
Edited By: Naomi Blair & Heather Berridge Manning

Copyright © 2021 by Fifth Ribb Publishing

All Rights Reserved. This book or any portion thereof may not be reproduced or used in any manner whatsoever without the express written permission of the publisher except for the use of brief quotations in a book review.

Printed in the United States of America

First Edition, 2021
ISBN: 978-1736789810

I dedicate this book to my muse, my husband Dr. Kurt Jackson and my amazing children: Miriam, Hadassah and Zebulun!

Hi! My name is Jaxson, and I'm six years old.

Everyone calls me Young Doc Jax because I want to be a doctor when I grow up, like Doc James.

4

Doc James is our family's physician. He takes care of everyone in our neighborhood. We all love Doc James.

Every Saturday morning at 11:00 am, I tune in and listen to *The Doc James Show* on the radio.

I get to ask him questions about our bodies. I love listening to Doc James.

Doc James even visits his patients at their home whenever they are not feeling well.

It's easy for him to do that because I live on a very small island called St. Croix.

St. Croix is awesome! The weather is always hot, and the beach is close to my house. Plus, our neighbors are like family because everyone knows each other.

I am one of Doc James' very special patients. I have asthma which sometimes makes me feel very sick. Doc James always comes to visit me to make me feel all better.

At times, I can't go out and play with my big brother, Jay, and my friends.

"It's ok, son. Don't be sad. Doc James will help you feel better soon," my Mommy and Daddy always say.

"It's not fair. I want to go out and play. I don't like being sick," I often cry.

I see Doc James, with his medicine bag, coming towards my house walking past Jay and my friends playing outside.

"It's ok, Young Doc Jax. What seems to be the problem?" Doc James asks as he enters my room.

"I want to go and play but I've been coughing all day. Sometimes I feel like I can't breathe," I explain.

"Let me examine you, and I'll get you back out to playing with your buddies as soon as I can," Doc James states.

"Ok, Doc James," I reply.

Doc James uses his stethoscope to listen to my lungs and hears wheezing sounds.

"What do you hear with your stethoscope?" I ask.

"Sounds like your asthma is acting up," states Doc James.

Then Doc James takes a tongue depressor and tells me to say, "Ahh."

"What do you see Doc James?" I spew out.

"I see your tonsils and they look fine. But it looks like you need to use your inhaler," he tells me.

Doc James gives me my inhaler which makes me start to feel better.

"Why does the inhaler make me feel better Doc James?" I ask.

"Great question! Your inhaler has medicine that makes your lungs work better, and that's why you feel better," Doc James explains.

"Aww Young Doc Jax. You'll be a great doctor too!" Doc James replies.

GLOSSARY:

Asthma - a health problem that makes it hard to breathe.

Inhaler - a handheld device used for breathing medicine into the lungs; used to treat asthma.

Lungs - baglike organs, or body parts, used for breathing.

Medicine - a pill or liquid used to prevent, cure, or relieve a disease.

Physician - another word for a medical doctor.

Stethoscope - a tool used to hear the sounds that the inside of the body makes.

Tongue depressor - a thin piece of wood that is rounded at both ends and that a doctor uses to press down on a patient's tongue when looking in the patient's throat.

Tonsils - lumps of tissues located on the back of your throat; they help to fight infection.

Wheezing - a whistling sound heard when someone's airway is partly blocked; a common asthma symptom.

Saint Croix (St. Croix) is an island in the Caribbean Sea. It is the largest of the United States Virgin Islands, and the capital is Christiansted. It was purchased by Denmark in 1753 and sold to the United States in 1917. By plane, it takes approximately 3 hours, 45 minutes to fly from Florida to St. Croix.

ABOUT THE AUTHOR:

Mother of 3, wife to Dr. Kurt T. Jackson, and Practice Manager of Jackson Eye Care, LLC., Kai Jackson resides in Montclair, NJ. Kai earned her BA from Long Island University, majoring in English Literature. It has always been a dream of hers to become an author. Drawing inspiration from her husband's childhood and the recent opening of their medical practice, she created the character Young Doc Jax to encourage young children of color to follow their dreams. Through this series, follow Young Doc Jax on his journey of becoming a doctor.

For publishing, Kai is represented by Fifth Ribb publishing.

ABOUT DR. KURT T. JACKSON:

Dr. Kurt Jackson is a practicing vitreo-retinal surgeon specializing in medical and surgical eye disease for more than a decade and is the founder of Jackson Eye Care, LLC. Dr. Jackson was born in Dominica, W.I. and moved to St. Croix when he was 3 months old. At 15, Dr. Jackson moved to Georgia where he attended high school and then enlisted in the U.S. Army after graduation. As a medic for four years and an eye technician for two years, Dr. Jackson received a US Army Achievement Medal, Commendation Medal, Good Conduct Medal, and a National Defense Medal.

Dr. Jackson attended Long Island University and graduated Valedictorian of the Class of 1998. He was accepted into the prestigious Albert Einstein College of Medicine where he graduated in 2003 with his medical doctorate degree. Happily married, Dr. Jackson has 3 children. In his spare time, Dr. Jackson enjoys spending quality time with his family and is active with his church. He is fluent in both English and Spanish and looks forward to serving the needs of his patients.

COMING SOON!

www.ingramcontent.com/pod-product-compliance
Lightning Source LLC
Chambersburg PA
CBHW051259110526
44589CB00025B/2885